TAPAS

BY ANN & LARRY WALKER

ILLUSTRATIONS BY AMY KOLMAN

CHRONICLE BOOKS

SAN FRANCISCO

Library of Congress Cataloging-in-Publication Data

Walker, Ann, 1944–
    Tapas / by Ann & Larry Walker ; illustrations by Amy Kolman.
        p.   cm.
    Includes index.
    ISBN 0-8118-0331-7
    1. Appetizers. 2. Cookery, Spanish.   I. Walker, Larry, 1936–
II. Title.
TX740.W234 1994
641.8'12—dc20   94-508
                                        CIP

Printed in Hong Kong.

Cover and interior design: Lory Poulson
Cover art: Amy Kolman

Distributed in Canada by Raincoast Books,
112 East Third Ave., Vancouver, B.C. V5T 1C8

10 9 8 7 6 5 4 3 2 1

Chronicle Books
275 Fifth Street
San Francisco, CA 94103

This book is for Montse Painous and Alberto Fornos, part of our extended Spanish family.

And for hundreds of barmen and restaurant staff across Spain who answered our questions with unfailing courtesy and good humor.

¡VIVA ESPAÑA!

CONTENTS

IN THE BEGINNING

The railroad was late coming to Spain, and the paved road even later. Well into the twentieth century, travel by horseback or coach was the most common way of getting from here to there. In the nineteenth century and earlier, the country was thick with bandits and those brave enough to take to the road often traveled in groups for mutual protection. As you may well imagine, the saddle-weary and nervous traveler was ready for a glass of wine upon arrival at one of the coaching inns, while fresh horses were saddled.

Hoping to make the most of these brief stops, innkeepers would rush into the courtyard with glasses of chilled sherry or hearty red table wine, urging the customers to drink up and order another "for the road." It is impossible to say just when and where the custom of placing a piece of bread over the glass originated. In Spanish, such a lid or covering is called a *tapa*, from the verb *tapar,* "to cover." Wherever and whenever this custom developed, it was a stroke of genius. The bread kept the dust, flies, and other unsavory debris swirling around the courtyard from settling into the wine. It also furnished a snack for the traveler, which encouraged another glass of wine, which was good for the innkeeper's bottom line—what modern retailers might call the "value-added system."

It didn't take long for an enterprising innkeeper to add a slice of ham or cheese to the bread as a further inducement to eat, drink, and run up a bigger bar bill. In time, the entire range of bar snacks became known as *tapas*. So, you see, that whole wonderful range of goodies we now call *tapas* was originally invented just to keep the flies out of the wine.

WHAT IS A TAPA?

When tapas became a culinary buzzword, we found many people confused over just what they are. It is still a common question, yet there is nothing strange or mysterious about tapas: tapas, or something like them, are found all over the world. The English call them starters; Americans call them appetizers; in France, they are *hors d'oeuvres;* in Canton, *dim sum;* in the Middle East, *mezze;* in Mexico, *antojitos;* in Italy, *antipasti.*

What distinguishes tapas from these other little dishes is more the spirit of the eater, not the food itself. Tapas reflect an unhurried approach; one lingers over tapas, they aren't simply fuel to keep the body functioning.

Tapas can be just about anything in small portions. At their simplest, the tapa may be only a plate of olives, perhaps a few slices of ham, a bit of cheese, a small serving of fried squid or grilled prawns; they also can be as elaborate as the cook's imagination and resources, as shown in such dishes as *Tortilla Española* or *Tartaletas de Salchichas y Caracoles.*

MEZZE

Along with many other good things—oranges, rice, spices—the Moors probably brought tapas to Spain. They didn't call them tapas, of course. They would have called them *mezze*, or some variation of that word. Common throughout the eastern Mediterranean and North Africa, a *mezze* (*mezé* in Greek) is simply a serving of small dishes, now commonly offered in bars and restaurants to accompany wine or the local *pastis*. The *mezze*, like the tapa, could be anything from a plate of olives to grilled prawns. As with the tapa, the exact food served as a *mezze* is less important than the social occasion. The *mezze*, like the tapa, is a way of life.

WHEN IS TAPA TIME?

Anytime at all is tapa time. In Spain, they are probably most common in the hour or so before dinner, say from 7:00 p.m. until 9:00 or 9:30 p.m. It is during this time that friends meet for a tapa or three before going on to dinner. There is always an abundant variety of tapas available and the more popular bars are crowded with happy eaters. Another popular time for tapas is about 4:00 p.m., known as "vermouth time," which may or may not have anything to do with vermouth. It simply means a small break in the late afternoon for a little bite of something and a glass of this or that, which is, in many cases, a white or red vermouth, on the rocks, or perhaps half of each. It might also be a small beer, a glass of wine, or a sherry. Ordinarily, the "vermouth" tapa is a simple cold tapa, such as grilled mushrooms or ham and cheese.

A more serious tapa opportunity is the *merenda,* which is a bit more elaborate than the vermouth. The *merenda* could even be a very simple meal of two or three small tapa plates. Like the vermouth tapa, these will often be cold plates or bar tapas, usually accompanied by wine or beer. The *merenda* is most often a mid-afternoon break and can even take the place of lunch. The origin of the word is interesting. It goes back to the Latin *merum,* meaning "pure," and is related to the modern Italian word *mero,* which has the particular meaning of a "pure wine," usually referring to an unbottled, homemade wine.

SPANISH HOURS

The Spanish do spend a lot of time at the table, but they don't eat a lot. Otherwise, Spain would be the world's most overweight nation and, in fact, one rarely sees a fat Spaniard.

Breakfast at 7:00 or 7:30 a.m. is light—a roll, coffee, or chocolate—often taken standing up at a snack bar. Agricultural workers will have a hearty snack at mid-morning but most office workers will have only a coffee, so they are truly hungry by lunch, which is late by our standards, 1:30 or 2:00 p.m. Lunch is usually the biggest meal of the day and can easily last two hours. However, if a large dinner is planned for the evening, a few tapas or the *merenda* will substitute for lunch. If, for some reason, lunch was early or business has limited the pleasures of the noonday table, there is always a tasty something to look forward to at "vermouth time." But most are back to work by 4:00 p.m. and work until 7:00 or 7:30 p.m. Then it is time for tapas before the evening meal, which could be a light dinner at home—maybe soup or a sandwich at 10:00 or 10:30 p.m., or a more elaborate dinner at a restaurant, which would begin about 11:00 p.m. and last until well past midnight.

This sort of schedule has left many wondering just when

LIFESTYLE

A tapa is a delicious morsel of food that defines a lifestyle as well as a culinary style. Tapas in Spain are almost always accompanied by wine, but they are as much about talking as they are about eating and drinking. The wine is, perhaps, the medium that holds the conversation, the friends, and the food together. The primary purpose of tapas is to talk to friends, to share the gossip of the day. Tapas are part of the shared communal life of the *pueblo* at the public level, a giggle between two good friends at a more private level.

the Spaniard sleeps. In fact, statistics compiled by the European Community indicate that the average Spaniard sleeps only about an hour less a day than most other Europeans.

The Spanish *siesta* does still exist, despite efforts to make the Spanish worker conform to other European or American work habits, but it isn't often used as nap time these days. More often, the long lunch breaks that are not given over to food are used as shopping time, an opportunity to run errands, read, or indulge in any number of other afternoon delights.

However, you may let the Spanish keep whatever hours they wish, and still enjoy the pleasures of tapas by adapting them to your schedule.

JUST HOW BIG IS A TAPA, ANYWAY?

Tapas come in two sizes, small and not-so-small. The small dishes are little more than a few bites, and several can be taken without threatening to spoil the dinner to come. In Spain, these little dishes are very often served cold, directly from the bar. Purists insist that these are the true tapas, the little dishes that were once given away in Spanish bars. A serving about twice the size of the small dishes is called a *ración*. It is often served hot (or at least warm) from the kitchen. The small dishes are more likely to be eaten in the late morning or early evening. The more substantial *ración* sometimes takes the place of lunch or serves as an early evening snack if dinner is going to be around midnight, which it may often be in Spain.

ABOUT THE RECIPES

In the course of teaching and talking about tapas, we have found a great curiosity and eagerness to learn about Spanish cuisine in general and about tapas in particular. There seems to be something about the concept that excites the imagination and inspires inventive cooks to reach for their aprons.

The tapa concept fits in well with our modern lifestyle with its emphasis on healthy cuisine. Many tapas make use of olive oil, which helps control cholesterol, in sharp contrast to many American snacks, which rely heavily on sugar, salt, and saturated fats. In addition, tapas are based on seafood or vegetables with only small amounts of lean, grilled meats. This is typical of the traditional Mediterranean diet, which is associated with low rates of heart disease and cancer.

The recipes in this book are authentic Spanish tapas, or tapas adapted for the American kitchen in those few cases where a particular ingredient might not be available. We would like to urge you to use them in a familiar way. Tapas need not be just a special-occasion treat; they can easily enter your everyday, Monday-through-Friday kitchen.

Finally, use these recipes as a Spanish cook would, as a working base useful for developing your own ideas—make them your own. Vary the ingredients and use what is available in your kitchen or market, as a Spanish cook would. We have made some menu suggestions which you can take as a guide for developing your own menus and occasions for tapas. They are user-friendly recipes with no special equipment needed, just a love of good food, shared with friends.

TAPAS AND WINE

SHERRY

Although it is of course possible to drink any wine you like with tapas, the quintessential tapas wine is sherry. If your idea of sherry is the sweet dreck that Aunt Sandy from Chicago puts away by the thimbleful during the holidays, we strongly urge you to revise your thinking. Unlike the heavily fortified sweet sherries common in the United States—which can be a bit like quaffing cough syrup—a slightly chilled, bone-dry *fino* or *manzanilla* sherry is light and lively on the palate and the perfect wine for a great many tapas. Dry sherries have a unique earthy flavor, combined with a salty finish (especially in the *manzanillas)*, that complements the salty, tangy flavor of scores of tapas, from a plate of olives, ham, or cheese, to fresh shellfish.

There are two basic kinds of sherry: *fino* and *oloroso*. All other sherries are variations of these two basic styles and both began life absolutely dry. Almost all sherries drunk with food are in the *fino* category—including *manzanilla*, a *fino* sherry from the town of Sanlúcar, and *amontillado*. Although *oloroso* may also be bottled dry, it is most likely to be found sweet. The sweetness comes from the addition of the juice of a very sweet grape called Pedro Ximinez. But since, for the most part, sweet sherry is not drunk with food (*amontillado* is often drunk with soup, but rarely served with tapas), we'll cut to the chase and go straight to the lovely topic of *fino* and *manzanilla,* surely the most refreshing wines made.

There is a cool earthiness to a chilled dry sherry that is haunting and unmistakable on the palate; it is exactly this quality that makes sherry such a good match with so many

foods, from simple to complex. There are few things to equal a grilled chicken eaten with a half-bottle of chilled *fino* at one of the many fiestas in a small village in Andalucía. Unless it might be a plate of grilled prawns, flecked with garlic, enjoyed on the beach at Sanlúcar with a glass of *manzanilla* from the barrel behind the bar, sherry which has traveled only a few hundred yards from its home in a nearby *bodega*.

The production of sherry differs in several major ways from the table wine most of us are accustomed to drinking. Sherry is made by a system called the *solera* method, in which sherries from different years are blended in a barrel to achieve a standard quality. The *solera* system can be quite elaborate, but in its most simple form, about 25 to 35 percent new sherry enters the system each year, with another 25 to 35 percent being bottled for shipment.

However, in some cases *soleras* may be over a century old. That doesn't mean the wine in the bottle is one hundred years old or older, but that a tiny (very tiny) fraction of the wine came from a barrel or a part of the *solera* that was established a century before.

What makes sherry utterly different from any other wine is the growth of wild yeast cells on the surface of the wine. This growth, called *flor* in Spanish because under a microscope the growth looks like tiny flowers, has traditionally been used by the winemakers to help determine the quality of the wine. If no *flor* appears, the wine becomes an *oloroso*, destined to be a dessert sherry—and some can be quite magnificent. If there is a healthy growth of *flor*, the wine is a *fino*. Although some still rely on the *flor* to determine the style of sherry, most modern *bodegas* make *fino* from the free-run juice that comes from the grapes before they are crushed, and make *oloroso* from the first and second crushings of the grapes, not waiting for the *flor* to develop. It happens sometimes that the free-run juice stubbornly refuses to grow *flor*, so it, too, becomes *oloroso*. This unique *flor*, or bloom, is found nowhere else in the world but the area of Spain centered around Jerez de la Frontera, the authentic sherry zone.

One reason sherry has failed to earn much respect in the United States is the way Americans drink it. Someone needs to take American wine consumers to one side and give them a few lessons in How to Drink Sherry. This is a good time to start.

Sherry should be drunk as fresh as possible; even the sweet sherries begin to fade quickly once the bottle is opened. And, ideally, the *finos* need to be consumed within a few hours of opening the bottle, at a temperature of between 50° and 55° F. In fact, sherry, considered the most delicate of wines, actually begins to lose its freshness as soon as it is bottled. To ensure freshness, try to get your local wine shop to find out when the sherry it sells was bottled and shipped. If your shopkeeper is unwilling to make that effort, perhaps you should consider another wine shop. *Fino* should be drunk within a year of bottling.

OTHER WINES

Of course, many wines other than sherry can match perfectly with the various flavors of tapas. The wine suggestions following each recipe are intended as just that—suggestions. There are no rules concerning food and wine, certainly not when it comes to tapas and wine. Well, there is one rule, actually. The wine should taste good to you.

Aside from sherry, let your palate be your guide, since the international world of wine is remarkably diverse and exciting, as are the flavors of Spanish tapas.

Salud.

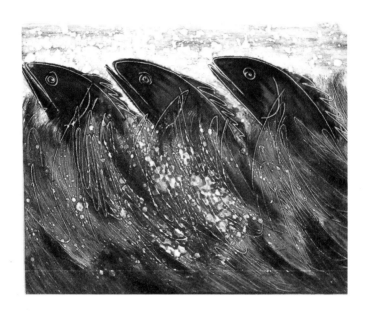

CHAPTER ONE

THE SEA

Spain, with both an Atlantic and a Mediterranean coast, is incredibly rich in seafood. The selection of fish and shellfish at the markets, even the inland markets, is truly amazing. Special trains leave from the country's main fishing ports to carry fresh seafood to the interior, where it can be bought within hours of leaving the sea. Some form of seafood is found in virtually every tapas bar in Spain, ranging from a seafood salad like the *Salpicon de Mariscos* (page 22) to simple grilled prawns.

When visiting Spain, one finds an abundance of fresh anchovies *(anchoa)* and sardines *(sardina)*, especially fried or grilled. Mackerel *(caballa)* is very good from the grill as is fresh tuna *(atún)*. One of the very best eating fish in Spain is monkfish *(rape)* which has a firm, sweet-flavored flesh.

There are many varieties of both fish and shellfish common to Spain that simply are not available in the United States. We have, in those cases, substituted fish or shellfish of similar texture or flavor.

If you live in an area where fresh fish or shellfish is seldom available, today's modern methods of freezing fresh-caught fish and shellfish assures top quality. Frozen fish and shellfish can be substituted, if necessary, in the following recipes.

MARINATED SHELLFISH SALAD

Salpicon de Mariscos

A zesty salad that can stand on its own as a light lunch
but is delicious as a tapa before dinner.

SERVES SIX TO EIGHT AS A TAPA, FOUR AS A LIGHT LUNCH

1 tablespoon fresh lemon juice
1 tablespoon sherry wine vinegar
1/2 cup extra-virgin olive oil
1/2 teaspoon each salt and freshly ground black pepper
1 bay leaf
1 medium onion, peeled and quartered
1/2 pound unshelled prawns
1/2 pound shelled scallops
1/2 pound cleaned squid tubes, cut into 1/2-inch rings
1 pound clams, scrubbed clean
3 gherkins, thinly sliced
2 tablespoons tiny capers
3 tablespoons minced fresh chives
1 red bell pepper, stemmed, seeded, and cut into 1/4-inch dice

To make the dressing, whisk together the lemon juice, vinegar,
olive oil, salt, and pepper in a small bowl and set aside.

In a large pot, bring 4 cups of water to a boil with the bay
leaf and onion. Peel the prawns and set aside. Add the shells to
the boiling water. Cook briskly 15 minutes. Strain, discarding
solids. Return the broth to a boil.

Add the prawns to the broth and cook until they turn a bright pink color, about 2 minutes (but keep an eye on them because they can overcook quickly). Remove prawns and set aside in a large bowl. Return the broth to a boil, add the scallops, and cook until just opaque, about 1 minute. Remove and add to the prawns. Return the broth to a boil, add the squid, and cook for 30 seconds. Remove and add to the prawns and scallops. When the broth is boiling again, add the clams and cook until they open. Remove the clams, set aside, and strain the broth to remove any grit. Remove the clams from their shells and add to the bowl of shellfish. Discard the shells. (See Note.)

Add the dressing, gherkins, capers, chives, and bell pepper to the shellfish. Toss until well combined. Refrigerate for 3 to 4 hours before serving, tossing occasionally.

To serve, pile the marinated shellfish onto a platter and serve with small plates, forks, and lots of good bread to dip into the delicious juices.

NOTE: It's a shame to throw away the rich cooking water from *Salpicon de Mariscos*. After it cools, pop it into the freezer for later use in seafood soups and sauces or as the basis for stock.

WINE SUGGESTIONS: A chilled *manzanilla* sherry is ideal. However, your favorite California Chardonnay, so long as it isn't too oaky, would also work well here.

SQUID SALAD

Ensalada de Calamares

Some form of squid salad is a standard in tapas bars all over
Spain. In this simple recipe, the addition of cilantro shows
Moorish or South American influence and would be common
in the Canary Islands or the south of Spain.

SERVES TEN

10 cloves garlic
1/2 bunch fresh parsley
1/2 bunch fresh cilantro
1/2 teaspoon toasted cumin seeds
1 tin (2 ounces) anchovy fillets, drained
1/2 teaspoon each salt and freshly ground black pepper
1/2 cup olive oil
1/4 cup red wine vinegar
Juice of 2 lemons
1 pound cleaned squid tubes and tentacles
1 each medium red and green bell pepper, stemmed,
   seeded, and sliced into thin strips
1 medium red onion, peeled and thinly sliced into rings

In a food processor or blender, grind together the garlic, parsley, cilantro, cumin, anchovies, salt and pepper. In a small bowl, combine the oil, vinegar, and lemon juice; with the motor running, gradually add to the herb mixture. Set the dressing aside in a bowl.

Bring a pot of salted water to a boil. Cut the squid tubes into 1/4-inch rings, leaving the tentacles whole. Blanch the squid in the boiling water for 30 seconds. Remove and immediately toss the cooked squid with the dressing. Fold in the peppers and onions and refrigerate overnight before serving.

WINE SUGGESTIONS: A *fino* sherry or a glass of *cava* would work well with this dish. A California Sauvignon Blanc, especially if it is on the herbal side, is another good option.

PAELLA SALAD

Ensalada de Paella

We discovered this dish one rainy Sunday afternoon in a small bar off the Plaza Mayor in Madrid. It is rather unusual, since *paella* is rarely served as a salad in Spain. It was served in mussel shells with a glass of delicious chilled rosé wine from vineyards near Toledo. The preparation looks complicated, but broken down into the following five-step program, it goes fairly fast and easily.

SERVES TWELVE AS A TAPA, SIX AS A FIRST COURSE, FOUR AS A LUNCH

1/2 pound unshelled mussels
1 cup dry white wine
1/2 pound unshelled prawns
1/2 pound cleaned squid tubes, cut into 1/2-inch rings
3 cloves garlic
1/2 teaspoon saffron threads
3/4 cup olive oil
2 tablespoons lemon juice
1 teaspoon salt
1/2 teaspoon ground white pepper
1 1/2 cups paella, arborio, or short-grain rice
1 cup fresh or frozen baby peas
*1 small or 1/2 large red bell pepper, stemmed,
    seeded, and thinly sliced lengthwise*
3/4 pound tomatoes, diced into small pieces

FIRST STEP: Wash and debeard the mussels. Bring the wine and 1 cup of water to a boil in a small stockpot. Either place the mussels in a steamer basket over the boiling liquid or drop them into it and cook just until the mussels are open. Remove the mussels and set aside. Bring the liquid back to a boil and drop in the prawns. Cook the prawns until they turn a bright pink color, about 1 to 2 minutes. Do not overcook. Remove the prawns and set aside. Return the liquid to a boil and add the squid rings. Cook for no more than 30 seconds. Remove the squid and set aside. Strain the cooking liquid to remove any grit. Measure the liquid and add water to bring it to 3 cups. Set aside.

SECOND STEP: To prepare the dressing, combine the garlic, saffron, and 1/4 cup of the oil in a blender and puree. With the motor running, add the remaining oil, lemon juice, salt, and pepper. Adjust seasonings to your taste. Set aside for the flavors to mingle while the rice cooks.

THIRD STEP: Bring the 3 cups of reserved liquid to a boil. Taste for salt and add an additional teaspoon if necessary (remember, the shellfish will also add salt). Pour in the rice and return to a boil. Cover, reduce heat to low, and cook 20 minutes.

FOURTH STEP: While the rice cooks, peel and devein the prawns and place in a nonreactive bowl. Drain any accumulated juices from the squid and add the squid to the prawns. Stir the dressing and add 1/4 cup to the prawns and squid. Remove and discard the top shell from each of the mussels. Drizzle a little dressing over each of the mussels. Set aside.

FIFTH STEP: Remove the rice from heat, uncover, and pour in the peas. Cover and let rest for 5 to 10 minutes. Toss with the remaining dressing, the peppers, and the tomatoes. Add the prawns and squid and toss. Arrange on a platter and garnish with the mussels. Serve at room temperature or slightly chilled.

WINE SUGGESTIONS: A crisp, dry Sauvignon Blanc from California or a dry rosé from the south of France or northern Spain would go well with this. Or for a slightly different effect, try a Beaujolais from France or a light (not white) Zinfandel from California.

SAFFRON

Saffron is made from the dried flower of *Crocus sativus*, a common Mediterranean plant. It takes between seventy and eighty thousand saffron flowers to produce one pound of the spice. The entire process, from picking to preparation, is labor intensive, so it isn't hard to understand why saffron is one of the most expensive cooking ingredients around. However, used properly, a little goes a long way and the cost per dish is quite minimal. Another reason to avoid overuse is that too much saffron imparts a bitter, medicinal flavor. Always buy threads of saffron, never the powder, which is easily adulterated with the addition of foreign materials. With the threads, what you see is what you get.

ASPARAGUS & SMOKED SALMON FINGERS

Batutas de Espárragos y Salmón Ahumado

We first met this rather elegant tapa in a *xampanyeria* in Barcelona. It makes an attractive dish to pass at a cocktail party, or a palate-pleasing first course for dinner.

SERVES SIX TO EIGHT AS A TAPA, FOUR TO SIX AS A FIRST COURSE

20 spears thin asparagus
10 thin slices smoked salmon, cut in half
All-purpose flour
2 eggs beaten with 1 tablespoon water
Bread crumbs for coating
Olive oil for frying

Break off the bottom third of the asparagus spears, leaving about 3 inches of the tops. In a small pot, steam the asparagus until tender but not limp, about 5 minutes. Twist one slice of the salmon around each asparagus spear.

Put flour, beaten eggs, and bread crumbs into separate, shallow dishes. Coat each spear with flour, then dip into the egg, and, finally, coat with the bread crumbs. Lay the coated asparagus spears on a plate and refrigerate for at least 45 minutes.

Heat 2 inches of olive oil in a deep-sided skillet. When hot but not smoking, cook the asparagus a few at a time until golden. Drain on paper towels and serve immediately.

WINE SUGGESTIONS: Champagne, a Spanish *cava*, or a big, buttery Chardonnay from California are ideal with this dish.

XAMPANYERIA

The *xampanyeria* (the *x* in Catalan is pronounced "ch") is an upscale Barcelona version of the tapas bar. The food is usually more elegantly presented at a *xampanyeria* and, although other wines are available, *cava*, Spanish sparkling wine, is the drink of choice. Some bars have as many as forty different *cavas* available for sampling. The decors of most *xampanyerias* have a somewhat glossy look that would be at home in Paris, London, or San Francisco, and the taped music is more likely to be English rock or American jazz than flamenco. They are very popular with Barcelona's younger set.

SCALLOPS ON THE HALF-SHELL WITH WHITE WINE SAUCE

Vieiras al Vino Blanco

This classic tapa is found all over Spain and makes a wonderful first course as well as an appetizer. For an authentic Spanish touch, serve the scallops in their shells, which are readily available at fine food shops or kitchen supply stores.

SERVES SIX AS A TAPA, FOUR AS A FIRST COURSE

2 tablespoons unsalted butter
1 medium onion, minced
1/4 pound fresh mushrooms, minced
1/2 teaspoon salt
1/4 teaspoon freshly ground black pepper
Pinch of nutmeg
1/4 cup brandy
1 cup dry white wine (See Wine Suggestions)
1/2 cup heavy cream
1 pound shelled scallops
1 tablespoon minced fresh parsley

Melt the butter in a large skillet. Add the onions and cook over low heat until very soft and golden, about 15 minutes. Stir in the mushrooms, season with salt, pepper, and nutmeg, and cook until the liquid that exudes from the mushrooms has evaporated. Pour in the brandy, stand back, and shake the pan to ignite. Cook until the flames subside. Pour in the wine and cook quickly over high heat until the liquid has reduced to a couple of tablespoons. Stir in the cream and heat through.

Add the scallops; stir and cook briefly until the scallops are cooked through. (This takes very little time, about 1 minute, but of course depends on the size of the scallops.)

Divide the scallop mixture among scallop shells or pour into a shallow casserole. If you want to add a golden touch to the dish, run the scallops under a preheated broiler for just a moment to toast the surface. Sprinkle with the minced parsley and serve immediately with small forks or toothpicks and crusty breads to *hacer una barca* ("make a boat") for scooping up all the lovely sauce.

WINE SUGGESTIONS: Serve the same wine used in the sauce. A full-bodied California Chardonnay would do nicely or, for a slightly leaner touch, try a crisp Vouvray from the Loire Valley of France, a wine made from the Chenin Blanc grape.

FISH FILLETS WITH CILANTRO-GREEN PEPPER SAUCE
Pescado Frito con Mojo Verde

You can find this "catch-of-the-day" fish dish all over Spain, including the Canary and Balearic Islands. As a tapa, it is normally a larger dish, a *ración*. Any firm-fleshed fish will work fine. Here we have suggested serving the tapa with the *Mojo Verde* sauce (page 107) typical of the Canary Islands, but it would also be delicious with the Catalan *Romesco* sauce (page 105).

2 pounds fresh cod, snapper, swordfish, or seabass fillets
1/2 cup all-purpose flour
1 teaspoon salt
1/2 teaspoon ground white pepper
1 teaspoon ground cumin
1/2 cup olive oil
1 recipe Mojo Verde, page 107

If there are any large bones in the fish, remove them. Cut the fish into 2-inch squares. Combine the flour and seasonings in a bag.

Heat the oil in a medium skillet. Shake the fish pieces in the bag with the seasonings. Shake off excess seasonings from the fish and lay the fish in the hot oil, cooking a few pieces at a time. Do not crowd the skillet or the fish will be soggy rather than crisp. When the fish is golden on both sides, remove and drain on paper towels.

The fish can either be coated with the *Mojo Verde* and served at room temperature, or served hot with the sauce on the side for guests to dip into or spoon over their servings.

WINE SUGGESTIONS: The challenge here is to match the smoky sharpness of the green sauce and let the fish worry about itself. A *fino* sherry would be our first choice, but a California Sauvignon Blanc would also be very good. For the daring, try a fresh, lively dry Chenin Blanc from California.

GREEN OLIVES STUFFED WITH ANCHOVIES

Aceitunas Rellenos con Anchoas

Although canned stuffed green olives are available in the United States, this homemade version really does taste better. All that's needed is a little patience. We find that a small glass of *fino* sherry for the cook makes the job go faster.

SERVES TEN TO TWELVE

40 medium pitted green olives
20 anchovy fillets, halved
2 tablespoons olive oil
1 tablespoon sherry wine vinegar
2 tablespoons minced fresh parsley
1/2 red bell pepper, cut into very fine strips

Drain and rinse the olives. Shake dry. Lay the olives out on a paper towel. Stuff each olive with half an anchovy and put aside.

In a nonreactive bowl, mix together the oil, vinegar, parsley, and bell pepper. Toss the olives with the dressing and refrigerate overnight. To serve, pour the olives and their dressing into a dish and serve with toothpicks.

WINE SUGGESTIONS: This is a classic *fino* sherry dish, as the saltiness of the stuffed olives matches well with the lean acidity of the sherry. A Sauvignon Blanc could work also.

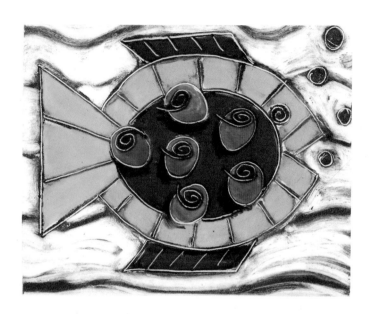

TUNA & OLIVE CROQUETTES
Croquetas de Atún y Aceitunas

Croquettes have been raised to an art form by the Spanish. They are at home in the posh restaurants of Barcelona and Madrid as well as the street-corner cafes of the small *pueblos*. Croquettes are ideal for leftovers, a quality dear to any busy cook's heart.

SERVES SIX TO EIGHT AS A TAPA, FOUR AS A FIRST COURSE

2 tablespoons unsalted butter
1 medium onion, minced
1/4 cup all-purpose flour
1 can (7 ounces) tuna, packed in water
Milk
Salt and ground white pepper
1/2 cup pimiento-stuffed green olives, chopped

Melt the butter in a small saucepan over medium heat. Add the onion and cook until soft. Stir in the flour and cook for 1 minute. Drain the liquid from the tuna into a measuring cup, reserving the tuna. Add enough milk to equal 1/4 cup liquid and whisk into the flour mixture, cooking and stirring over low heat until thickened, about 1 minute. Season with the salt and pepper to taste and stir in the reserved tuna and the olives.

Pour the contents of the saucepan onto a flat plate and cover with waxed paper. Refrigerate until cold.

Follow the directions for shaping, coating, and frying the croquettes in the recipe for Ham and Cheese Croquettes on page 93.

WINE SUGGESTIONS: Perfect with a California Chardonnay or a dry white wine from Catalonia in Spain.

HACER UNA BARCA

The Spanish hate to see a delicious sauce go to waste, which is one reason that bread, especially a crusty bread, is found at virtually every Spanish meal. There is a Spanish idiom, *hacer una barca*, which means "to make a boat." The idea is that you "sail" your boat of bread around the plate, taking on the sauce.

SAMPLE TAPAS MENUS

Tapas can fit into many situations, from casual picnics
to more formal entertaining events at home.

FINGER-FOOD TAPAS

Green Olives Stuffed with Anchovies, page 36.
Asparagus and Smoked Salmon Fingers, page 30.
Grilled Bread with Fresh Tomato, page 84.
Meatballs in Garlic Sauce, page 65.
Pork Skewered with Figs and Prunes, page 52.
Stuffed Breast of Chicken with Orange Mayonnaise,
on a baguette, page 74.

TAILGATE TAPAS

Crescent-Shaped Pastries Filled with
Cumin-Scented Chicken, page 77.
Eggs in Overcoats, page 62.
Fava Bean and Rice Salad, page 48.
Fish Fillets with Cilantro–Green Pepper Sauce,
page 34.

PICNIC TAPAS

Fire-Roasted Peppers with Minced Garlic,
Posada de Villa, page 50.
Avocado Cream Toasts, page 88.
Potato and Onion Cake, page 91.
Sweet Red Pepper, Tomato, and Hazelnut Sauce,
page 105, served with grilled chicken pieces.

TAPAS BUFFET

Cabbage Rolls Stuffed with Pork, Raisins,
and Pine Nuts, page 54.
Kidneys in Sherry Sauce, page 68.
Grilled Mushrooms with Garlic and Parsley
Sauce, page 86.
Herbed Veal and Sausage Skewers, page 57.
Marinated Shellfish Salad, page 22.

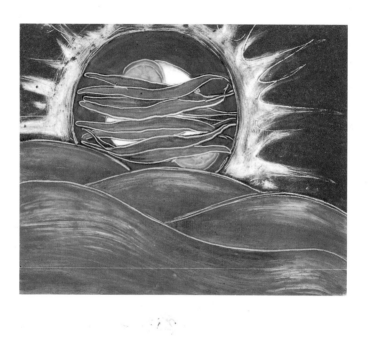

CHAPTER TWO

THE LAND

The first thing that strikes a visitor strolling through one of Spain's public markets is the freshness and quality of the vegetables and fruits. The Spanish cook does more than pay lip service to the oft-heard credo, "use the best, fresh local produce." Many top restaurant chefs, such as Pedro Subijana, the owner and chef of one of the world's great restaurants, Akelarre in San Sebastián, start their day at 6 a.m. in the local market. Subijana will design the day's dinner specials based on what he finds in the market.

But it isn't only the professionals who pay attention. The home cook is just as stringent in his or her requirements. One example: Although Spanish farmers have learned that they can harvest underripe tomatoes and ship them to northern Europe, for the home market, the tomatoes must be vine ripe or no one will buy them and they will rot in the market stalls.

In addition to the quality, the abundance of produce is also striking. In Spanish markets, there is always something fresh from the warm gardens of Andalucía and the Levant coast south of Valencia. During summer season there is every type of bean imaginable from the cooler gardens of the Rioja region and northern Spain. Tropical fruits are air-shipped from the Canary Islands and displayed beside local winter vegetables such as turnips and beets in the local markets in Catalonia.

The message here is not that you have to do your shopping in Spain, but do take advantage of what is fresh and seasonal.

Plan menus and dishes around what is available and shop early and often at local farmers' markets or green markets, which are springing up across the United States.

Vegetables are treated with respect in Spain, not simply as a means to decorate the plate. But it is the meats that we miss, especially the marvelous hams of Spain. Each region and each village offers special air-cured hams that can only be found on the spot. The pigs are fed distinctive diets, varying from one area to another, that give the hams their marvelous flavors. A thin slice or two of the local ham, served with a crusty white bread, is certainly the most common tapa in Spain.

Pork of any sort is popular throughout Spain as it is the cheapest and usually the tastiest meat available. Although, having said that, lamb seems to turn up quite often in the Spanish kitchen. What we call spring lamb, the Spanish call *cordero pascual.* It is butchered between three months and one year and is always range fed. When you visit Spain, look for *cordero lechal,* which means "milky lamb." This is baby lamb that is under three months old and still nursing; it has a very delicate flavor.

Cabrito, or baby goat, is a common meat in Spain. It is similar to *cordero lechal* but somewhat more flavorful. In the country you might find *carne de cabra,* which is older goat with meat similar to mutton.

Beef is not as popular in Spain as in the United States and when eaten it is usually in the form of veal, or *tenera añojo,* literally a yearling. Animals slaughtered for veal in Spain are generally about one year old, and we believe the quality of the meat is better since the animals are kept on pasture and not confined to small pens, as they are in the United States.

Chicken is common in the cities, less so in the country where egg production is more important. In addition to turkey and duck, guinea fowl, quail, partridge, pheasant, and squab are also frequent visitors to the Spanish table.

Rabbit is also common, especially grilled rabbit, and is often prepared using the same recipes as chicken. Most rabbit in the city markets has been raised domestically, but in the country you might find wild rabbit or hare.

As tapas, most meat dishes become *raciós* or the larger plates. They are often served on skewers, or *pinchos,* as in the *Pinchos de Cerdo* recipe on page 52.

PROSCIUTTO

Prosciutto, an air-dried Italian ham commonly served thinly sliced for an appetizer, is rather expensive. For use in cooking, however, look at your local deli for the much more affordable end pieces. Prosciutto adds wonderful flavors to beans, omelets, stews, and salads, such as the Fava Bean and Rice Salad on page 48.

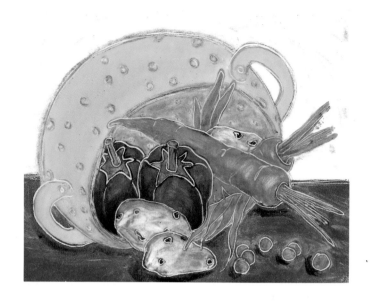

RUSSIAN SALAD
Ensalada Rusa

Found everywhere in Spain, this upscale version of potato salad can serve as a tapa, a *ración*, or a light lunch. There are many variations of the basic recipe, and we have included some below.

SERVES EIGHT TO TEN AS A TAPA, FOUR TO SIX AS A LIGHT LUNCH

1 pound russet potatoes, peeled and cut into ¹/2-inch dice
1 cup tiny frozen peas
1 large carrot, peeled and cut into ¹/4-inch dice
1 cup green beans, ends removed, cut into ¹/2-inch lengths
1 medium red bell pepper, stemmed, seeded,
   and cut into ¹/2-inch dice

1 tablespoon minced fresh parsley

1/2 cup minced pimiento-stuffed green olives

1/2 teaspoon salt

1 cup good-quality mayonnaise

2 teaspoons red wine vinegar

1 teaspoon Dijon-style mustard

2 hard-cooked eggs

Bring enough salted water to fully cover potatoes to a boil in a large pot, such as a spaghetti cooker with an insert that makes it easier to remove the vegetables after they are cooked.

Cook the potatoes in the water until tender; remove, draining well. Put the potatoes into a large bowl. Bring the water to a boil again, add the peas, and cook for 1 minute. Remove the peas and add to the bowl of potatoes. In the same water, cook the carrot and green beans until tender. Drain and add to the other vegetables.

Stir the red pepper, parsley, and olives into the vegetables. In a small bowl, mix together the salt, mayonnaise, vinegar, and mustard and fold into the vegetables. Taste for seasoning and add more salt and black pepper if you think it needs it.

Arrange the salad on a platter and garnish with wedges of egg. Refrigerate for 1 hour before serving.

VARIATIONS: Fold into the salad one of the following: 1 cup of canned tuna, drained and flaked; 1 cup of boiled prawns or tiny bay shrimp; or 1 cup of minced baked ham.

WINE SUGGESTIONS: A crisp, fruity Gewürztraminer would be good with this. A glass of sparkling wine wouldn't go wrong, either, but then it rarely does.

FAVA BEAN & RICE SALAD
Ensalada de Favas con Arròs

Rice and bean salads are popular all over the Mediterranean.
Fresh mint brightens this one with a lively, almost exotic
touch. The fava, or broad bean, is actually a cousin of the pea,
although it looks somewhat like a lima bean. They are best in
the late spring or early summer, when still small and tender.

SERVES TEN

1 thick slice white bread, crust removed
1/4 cup red wine vinegar
3 cloves garlic, minced
1/2 cup olive oil
6 anchovy fillets
1/4 cup minced fresh parsley
1 teaspoon minced fresh thyme
1 teaspoon each salt and freshly ground black pepper
1/2 cup fresh mint leaves, torn into small bits
1/4 pound Spanish ham or prosciutto, shredded (see Note)
2 cups short-grain rice
2 pounds unshelled fava beans

In a small bowl, soak the bread in the vinegar. Squeeze the
bread dry over the bowl, reserving the vinegar. Put the bread
and garlic in a blender or food processor. Pour in the vinegar
and, with the motor running, gradually add the olive oil. Add
the anchovies, parsley, thyme, salt, and pepper and process to
combine. Pour this dressing into a large bowl. Fold in the mint
and the prosciutto.

In a large pot, bring 3 quarts salted water to a boil. Add the rice to the water and continue to cook, uncovered, at a rapid boil until the rice is tender, about 15 minutes.

Meanwhile, bring a large saucepan of salted water to a boil. Shell the beans, add to the saucepan, and cook until tender. The younger they are the quicker they will cook, so the cooking time will vary. (In general, it is always better to test for doneness rather than watch the clock, whatever you are cooking.) Drain the beans and toss with the dressing.

Drain the rice and rinse under cold water. Toss the rice with the favas and dressing. Taste for seasoning. Allow the salad to rest at room temperature for 1 hour before serving.

NOTE: Although we have called for prosciutto in this recipe, Spanish hams are now being imported into the United States for the first time. Spanish ham, if it is available in your area, would be our preference.

WINE SUGGESTIONS: Favas and Riesling always seem a natural combination, but Sauvignon Blanc, a really crisp, fruity version, would also serve well.

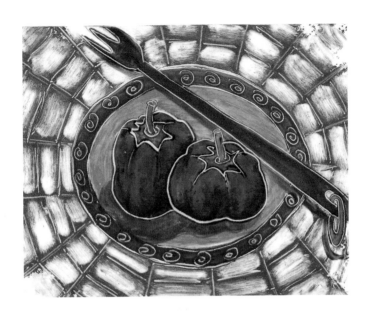

FIRE-ROASTED PEPPERS WITH MINCED GARLIC, POSADA DE VILLA

Pimientos Rojos Asados con Picadillo de Ajo, Posada de Villa

We first had this simple, inviting dish at the Posada de Villa
in Madrid, where it is a house specialty. The posada, on the
old coach road to Toledo, is a popular staging area for a night
of "doing tapas" around the Plaza Mayor, the center of old
Madrid. This delicious dish will get any evening off to a good
start. At its best if the peppers are roasted over a charcoal fire,
it is still yummy if you use a gas range.

SERVES SIX TO TEN

2 pounds firm red bell peppers
2 large cloves garlic, minced
¼ cup extra-virgin olive oil
Pinch salt
1 tablespoon very finely minced fresh parsley

Roast the peppers over a charcoal fire until blistered. Alternatively, put them under a broiler or skewer with a fork and hold over a gas flame until the outsides of the peppers are charred. After blistering them, put the peppers into a plastic bag and let them sweat for 10 minutes to make it easier to remove the skin. When cool enough to handle, remove the skins and stem and seed the peppers. Tear the peppers into strips and lay on a platter.

Sprinkle the garlic over the peppers. Drizzle the peppers with the olive oil. Sprinkle with the salt and parsley and let sit at room temperature for 30 minutes before serving.

WINE SUGGESTIONS: Delicious with sherry but also good with a medium-rich California Chardonnay.

PORK SKEWERED WITH FIGS & PRUNES

Pinchos de Cerdo con Higos Secos y Ciruelas

This is a substantial tapa that with a dish of rice could easily be a main course. The use of figs and prunes with pork marks this as a very old dish, probably a Mediterranean favorite during the days of the Roman Empire.

SERVES EIGHT TO TEN AS A TAPA, FOUR TO SIX AS A MAIN COURSE

1 pound lean boneless pork loin, cut into 36 cubes
9 dried figs, stemmed and cut in half
18 pitted prunes
1/8 teaspoon each ground cinnamon, cloves, salt, and pepper
1 1/2 cups apple juice or cider

Put the pork into a nonreactive bowl. Add the figs, prunes, seasonings, and apple juice. Cover and marinate in the refrigerator for 3 to 4 hours or overnight.

Remove the pork and fruit from the marinade, reserving the marinade. For each of eighteen 6- to 8-inch wooden or metal skewers, skewer a piece of pork, then a prune, then another piece of pork, and top with half a fig. Continue skewering until all eighteen have been completed.

Bring the marinade to a boil in a nonreactive skillet large enough to hold all of the skewers. Add the skewers, cover, reduce heat, and cook for 10 minutes. Remove the cover and continue to cook, turning the skewers from time to time, until the sauce is a sticky syrup. Serve immediately.

WINE SUGGESTIONS: The flavors here call out for a California Pinot Noir, a lively Beaujolais, or, best of all, a young Rioja.

CABBAGE ROLLS STUFFED WITH PORK, RAISINS, & PINE NUTS

Col Relleno con Cerdo, Pasas y Piñones

Cold-weather cabbage doesn't fit the image of sunny Spain, but from Seville to Barcelona and all points in between, cabbage is enjoyed in many delicious and creative ways. These cabbage rolls are a Catalan specialty, from the island of Majorca.

SERVES SIX TO EIGHT

1 medium head green cabbage
2 tablespoons olive oil
1 medium onion, minced
2 cloves garlic
1/4 cup pine nuts
1/4 cup raisins
3 ounces mild Italian sausage,
   casing removed and meat crumbled
3/4 pound boneless pork loin, minced
1/2 cup dry white wine
1/2 cup bread crumbs
1 teaspoon paprika
1/2 teaspoon each salt and freshly ground black pepper
2 large tomatoes, grated (see page 67)
2 cups chicken stock or 1 cup chicken stock
   and 1 cup dry white wine

Bring a large pot of salted water to a boil. With a small knife, remove the hard core from the cabbage. Cook the whole cabbage in the salted water for 15 minutes, then remove it from the water and let sit until cool enough to handle. Carefully remove the outer leaves, keeping them whole. Lay out the whole leaves on your work surface; shred the remaining smaller, inner leaves and set aside.

Heat the olive oil in a large skillet. Add the onion and garlic and cook until they begin to soften. Add the pine nuts and raisins and cook until the raisins plump. Stir in the reserved shredded cabbage leaves and cook over medium-high heat for 5 minutes or until the leaves are very limp and turning dark.

Add the sausage and minced pork to the skillet. Pour in the wine, increase the heat, and bring to a boil. Reduce heat to medium-low and cook, covered, for 10 minutes. Remove the lid. If there is still a lot of liquid remaining, increase the heat and reduce the liquid to about 1/4 cup. Stir in the bread crumbs, paprika, salt, and pepper.

Preheat the oven to 375° F.

Divide the meat mixture among the whole cabbage leaves. You can overlap leaves if necessary to make them large enough to fill. You will want 8 to 10 rolls, roughly 2 inches by 3 inches each. Tuck and roll the cabbage rolls and place seam sides down in one layer in a baking dish.

In a bowl, combine the grated tomatoes with the stock and lightly season with salt and pepper to taste. Pour the mixture over the cabbage rolls and bake in the preheated oven for 50 minutes.

Although the rolls can be served as soon as they come out of the oven, it is better to let them rest for about a half hour before serving. They hold together better and the flavors come through more distinctly as a result.

WINE SUGGESTIONS: Cabbage and Sauvignon Blanc make a good team, but we also like to serve a just off-dry California Riesling with this dish.

HERBED VEAL & SAUSAGE SKEWERS

Pinchos de Ternera y Salchichas a la Hierbabuena

This is a specialty of the Restaurante Hierbabuena
in Toledo, one of a number of exciting new restaurants
in that city. The use of veal and sausage together is
traditional, but the herbs give the dish a fresh, appealing
flavor. Note that in Spain, the veal is more mature than
in the United States, usually one to two years old, and
pasture fed, which gives it more flavor.

SERVES FOUR TO SIX

1 pound boneless veal, cut into 24 cubes
1 pound mild Italian link sausages, cut into 24 rounds
1 cup dry or slightly sweet white wine
$1/2$ cup combination of fresh thyme, oregano,
*   and lemon sage or regular sage leaves*

Using twelve 6-inch metal or wooden skewers, alternate 2
pieces each of veal and sausage on each of the skewers. Choose
a flat skillet that will accommodate all of the skewers, not necessarily in one layer, so that they are not sticking over the edge of
the pan. Heat the skillet over medium heat and cook the skewers for about 1 minute, turning them so all sides are seared.

Pour in the wine and sprinkle the herbs over the skewers.
Cover the skillet and cook over low heat for about 15 minutes.
Uncover and continue to cook, turning the skewers until they
are nicely glazed with the sauce, about 2 to 3 minutes. Serve hot.

WINE SUGGESTIONS: Perfect with Spanish Rioja or a big red wine from Catalonia. Pinot Noir would also work well, as would a not-too-heavy Cabernet Sauvignon, perhaps from Chile.

SAUSAGE & SNAIL TARTLETS
Tartaletas de Salchichas y Caracoles

This is a variation on a popular appetizer from the ancient
city of Llerida in Catalonia, where it is featured during
the annual spring snail festival. The variant here is that in
Llerida, the snails would always be fresh, never canned.
Live snails are commonly offered in the markets of Spain,
and the Spanish have found many delicious ways to serve
these tasty little bites, which too often are shunned in the
United States. The common garden snail in this country
is *very* edible indeed, especially after a diet of cornmeal
for a week or ten days.

The tartlet shells used here can be filled with other
goodies as well. After baking, you can fill them cold and
serve at room temperature or they can be filled and reheated
in the oven. Or, if you fill them with a raw custard-based
filling, it's not necessary to cook them first; just fill the
unbaked shells and cook for about twenty minutes
instead of ten.

YIELD: About 40 tartlets, depending on the size of the pan (most tartlet pans make twelve 1½-inch tartlets, although some pans make six 2-inch tartlets).

TARTLET PASTRY

4 ounces (8 tablespoons) cold unsalted butter
1½ cups all-purpose flour
1 egg
Dash of salt and cayenne pepper
1 tablespoon ice water

Preheat oven to 400° F.

Cut the butter into small pieces. Pour the flour into the work bowl of food processor. Add the butter and pulse to combine with the flour until smooth. Add the egg, seasonings, and water, pulse twice more, then whirl to form a ball.

For each tartlet, break off about 1 teaspoon of dough (the amount will vary depending on the size of the tartlet mold) and press into a nonstick tartlet mold. The dough should fit evenly over the bottom and the sides of the mold. The exact size of the mold isn't really important; the critical point is that the dough be stretched and pressed very thin to keep the tartlet from having a floury taste, whether the mold is 1½ inches in diameter or larger. Repeat with the remaining dough.

Place the molds on a baking sheet and bake the tartlets until golden brown, about 10 to 12 minutes. Turn the tartlets out of the molds and when cool, pack them in an airtight container. They will keep at room temperature for 1 week and can be frozen for up to 6 months.

FILLING

2 tablespoons balsamic vinegar
1/2 cup cream
1 tablespoon seeded-style mustard
1 tablespoon olive oil
1 medium onion, minced
3 cloves garlic, minced
1/2 pound Italian-style sausage,
   casing removed and meat crumbled
1/2 cup red wine
12 canned snails, minced
Salt and pepper

In a small bowl, combine the vinegar, cream, and mustard and set aside.

Heat the olive oil in a medium skillet. Slowly cook the onion and garlic over low heat until limp and golden. Stir in the sausage and cook for 5 minutes. Pour in the red wine and cook over high heat until dry. Pour off any excess oil.

Add the cream mixture to the skillet and cook to thicken slightly. Stir in the snails and season to taste with salt and pepper. Cook for a few minutes longer to further thicken the sauce and heat the snails.

Pour the mixture into the baked tartlet shells just before serving. Serve hot. If you feel it necessary, the filled tartlets can be reheated in the oven at 400° F.

WINE SUGGESTIONS: This dish is delicious with a dry Alsatian Gewürztraminer or a spicy California Sauvignon Blanc. For those who insist on drinking red, a California Merlot, full of fruit and flavor, is just the ticket.

EGGS IN OVERCOATS

Huevos con Gabárdinos

Students of the cuisine of the British Isles will notice a very strong similarity here to that famous English tapa, Scotch Eggs.

SERVES SIX TO TWELVE

7 medium eggs
1 tablespoon unsalted butter
¹/2 cup plus 1 tablespoon all-purpose flour
¹/2 cup milk
¹/4 teaspoon each salt and freshly ground black pepper
1 teaspoon Dijon-style mustard
¹/2 cup ground ham
Grating of nutmeg
¹/2 cup fine, dry bread crumbs
1 cup olive oil for frying

Put 6 of the eggs into a small saucepan and cover with cold water. Bring to a boil. Reduce to low heat and cook for 10 minutes. Remove from the heat and let sit for 5 minutes in the hot water.

Peel the eggs and cut in half lengthwise. Carefully remove the yolks and put them into a bowl. Cool the whites in the refrigerator.

Melt the butter in a small saucepan. Stir in 1 tablespoon of the flour and cook for about 1 minute. Whisking constantly, pour in the milk all at once. Continue whisking the sauce and cook until thickened, but do not allow to scorch. Season with salt and pepper.

Add the white sauce to the yolks and mash together. Stir in the mustard, ham, and nutmeg. Fill each egg white half to overflowing with the filling. Put two halves together and smooth out the seam between them with your fingers. Repeat with the remaining filling and whites.

Beat the remaining egg with 1 tablespoon cool water. Put the beaten egg, the bread crumbs, and the remaining $1/2$ cup flour into three separate, shallow bowls.

Dip an egg in the flour and coat well, then dip into the beaten egg. Finally, coat the egg thoroughly with the bread crumbs. Repeat with the remaining eggs. Put the eggs on a dish and refrigerate for at least 30 minutes. (If you wish, you can stop at this point and wait until the next day to cook the eggs.)

To fry the eggs, heat the oil in a medium deep-sided skillet (a deep-fat fryer can also be used). When the oil is hot but not smoking, fry the eggs until golden on all sides. Drain the eggs on paper towels. Let the eggs cool for 5 to 10 minutes. Cut in half and serve on a platter. The eggs can be served hot or at room temperature.

WINE SUGGESTIONS: These tasty bites are delicious with a glass of sparkling wine or a fresh, fruity white wine such as a California Chenin Blanc or a Sancerre from France.

MEATBALLS IN GARLIC SAUCE
Albóndigas al Ajillo

Don't be afraid of the garlic in this tapa, which takes meatballs out of the blah zone forever. This wonderfully warming winter dish can be frozen after cooking and reheated in a microwave.

SERVES TEN

3 tablespoons olive oil
2 heads garlic (about 20 to 24 cloves), peeled and left whole
Three 1-inch slices French bread
1 pound ground beef or any combination
    of ground veal, pork, and beef
4 tablespoons minced fresh parsley
1 teaspoon salt
1/2 teaspoon freshly ground black pepper
1/4 teaspoon nutmeg
1 large egg
All-purpose flour for coating
1 1/2 cups beef or chicken broth or a combination
    of broth and wine (the exact combination isn't
    important, as long as it adds up to 1 1/2 cups)
2 medium tomatoes

Heat 2 tablespoons of the olive oil in a skillet and add all but 3 or 4 cloves of the garlic. Cook until golden and remove. Toast 1 slice of the bread in the remaining oil. Break up the toasted bread and grind together with the cooked garlic in a blender or food processor. Reserve.

In a shallow bowl, soak the remaining 2 bread slices in water to cover, then squeeze dry. Mince the remaining cloves of garlic and combine in a large bowl with the soaked bread, meat, 2 tablespoons of the parsley, salt, pepper, nutmeg, and egg. Work the mixture with your hands until well mixed. Form into cocktail-sized balls. Toss the meatballs with the flour in a shallow bowl to coat. Shake off excess flour.

Heat the remaining tablespoon of oil in a large skillet, add the meatballs, and cook over medium heat until browned on all sides. Pour the stock over the meatballs. Cut the tomatoes in half and, using a grater, hold a tomato half in your hand and grate directly into the skillet. Discard the skin (see sidebar, following page). Stir in the reserved ground garlic-bread mixture. Cover and simmer for 30 minutes. If the sauce is still too thin, uncover the skillet, raise the heat, and cook until thickened.

Sprinkle the remaining 2 tablespoons of parsley over the meatballs and sauce and serve immediately, with toothpicks.

WINE SUGGESTIONS: The wine here can be "big," but it should have enough supple fruitiness to blend with the rich flavors of the dish. A California Merlot or a red wine from Rioja would be good.

PEELING TOMATOES

It isn't necessary to avoid all those recipes that call for the time-consuming chore of peeling and seeding tomatoes. Thanks to a technique we learned from a Spanish chef on one of our first visits to the country, peeling tomatoes is no longer drudgery. We were in the chef's restaurant kitchen after dinner, asking a few questions, when we suddenly noticed what the chef was doing. He was cutting tomatoes in half, then grating the pulp into a bowl until there was nothing left but the skin, which he discarded. He had "peeled" a tomato in about 15 seconds flat. You can also deseed the tomatoes simply by using a small knife to pop out the seeds after grating.

KIDNEYS IN SHERRY SAUCE
Riñónes a la Jerezana

Paradors, the state-operated tourist hotels in Spain, are not only a good place to hunt down special foods of the region, but they also are often situated on spectacular sites, like the Parador in the beautiful mountain town of Arcos de la Frontera in Andalucía, which overlooks a dramatic mountain landscape. Perhaps it has something to do with the view from the Parador's dining terrace, but the kitchen there does an especially delicious version of this common Andalus tapa. When friends in California tasted our re-creation of the dish, they agreed it was delicious but said Americans wouldn't eat kidneys. We disagree. We think American cooks are the most daring and adventurous in the world.

SERVES FOUR TO EIGHT

1 pound veal kidneys
2 tablespoons olive oil
2 cloves garlic, peeled
1 thick slice white bread, cut into large cubes
1 medium onion, minced
1 cup dry fino *sherry (see Wine Suggestions)*
1/4 teaspoon each salt and freshly ground black pepper
Minced fresh parsley for garnish

Clean, skin, and remove the fat and hard white part of the kidneys. Cut into ½-inch rounds. Heat 1 tablespoon of the olive oil in a small skillet or *cassuela* over medium heat. Put 1 clove of the garlic in to brown. Add 4 kidney rounds and the bread cubes and cook, stirring occasionally, until the bread is golden. Pour the contents of the skillet into a blender and purée with 1 cup of water. Set aside.

In the same skillet, heat the remaining tablespoon of olive oil. Mince the remaining clove of garlic and add with the onion to the skillet. Slowly cook over low heat until soft and beginning to turn a brownish color, about 15 minutes.

Stir in the remaining kidneys and increase the heat. Pour in the sherry and cook on high heat for 2 minutes. Stir in the puréed bread-kidney mixture and the salt and pepper. Reduce the heat and cook until the sauce has thickened. Serve immediately, lightly sprinkled with minced parsley.

NOTE: The kidneys will be tough if cooked too long or allowed to sit in the hot sauce. If you do not plan on serving the kidneys at once, remove the kidneys, onions, and sauce and store in the refrigerator. To serve, reheat the sauce, add the kidneys and onions, and heat through.

WINE SUGGESTIONS: It should be the chilled *fino* sherry used in the sauce, so make sure you buy a bottle good enough to drink. But if the cook finished off the bottle before serving time, a glass of Spanish *cava* would also work well.

SWEETBREADS WITH MUSHROOMS & BACON

Mollejas Bar Nicolas

We discovered this tapa at the Bar Nicolas in the wonderful old Roman city of Mérida in Extremadura. We had been out in a cold drizzle all morning visiting a Gypsy camp under the old Roman bridge (still in use) and were in need of warming nourishment. This friendly, flavorful dish was perfect. Although sweetbreads are not found in everyone's refrigerator, once you try this, they'll certainly be in yours more regularly. This tapa is substantial enough to have before a late-dinner *racion* or as a midday tapa. Note that part of this dish can be prepared the day before, if you wish.

SERVES SIX TO EIGHT AS A TAPA, FOUR AS A FIRST COURSE

l pound veal or lamb sweetbreads
3 teaspoons salt
Juice of 1 lemon
3 thin slices bacon
3 cloves garlic, minced
2 tablespoons all-purpose flour
1/2 teaspoon freshly ground black pepper
2 tablespoons olive oil
1/2 pound fresh button mushrooms, stemmed
2 or 3 tablespoons chopped fresh parsley for garnish

Put the sweetbreads in a bowl of cold water to cover and add 2 teaspoons of the salt. Refrigerate for an hour or two. Drain, rinse under cold water, and place in a saucepan with enough water to cover. Add 1 tablespoon of the lemon juice. Bring to a boil and cook for 10 minutes. Drain, reserving the cooking liquid, and plunge the sweetbreads into ice water to halt the cooking. Remove the filmy skin from the sweetbreads and separate into nickel-sized bits. (At this point, they can be refrigerated for use the next day or you can continue making the recipe.)

In a medium skillet, cook the bacon until it begins to brown. Add the minced garlic and cook for half a minute. Remove the garlic and bacon and set aside. When slightly cooled, crumble the bacon. Discard the fat.

Toss the sweetbreads in a shallow bowl with the flour, pepper, and remaining teaspoon salt. Wipe the skillet clean and heat the olive oil over medium heat. Cook the sweetbreads in small batches until golden brown. Drain on paper towels.

Add the mushrooms to the skillet. Sprinkle lightly with additional salt and pepper. Pour in 1 cup of the reserved cooking liquid. Stir and cook over medium heat for about 5 minutes. Return the sweetbreads, bacon, and garlic to the skillet. Stir in the remaining lemon juice. Cook over low heat until the sauce thickens. Sprinkle lightly with parsley and serve immediately.

WINE SUGGESTIONS: This is a very flavorful dish that can take a red wine with some zip, such as a Rioja from Spain or a Zinfandel from California. Oddly enough, the flavor of the sweetbreads also goes quite well with a dry Riesling from Alsace or California.

MUSHROOM STEMS

When stemming fresh mushrooms (as in the recipe for *Mollejas Bar Nicolas* on page 71), toss the stems into a plastic bag and put in the freezer. You can keep adding stems to the bag and take them out as needed to use in stocks, sauces, or soups that don't require whole mushrooms. In the Spanish kitchen (as in any well-run kitchen), nothing is ever wasted.

STUFFED BREAST OF CHICKEN WITH ORANGE MAYONNAISE

Rollos de Pollo con Salsa de Naranja

This multipurpose dish can work as a tapa, a picnic treat, or a cold first course. The use of mayonnaise indicates that it probably originated in northern Spain, where the use of mayonnaise is common, particularly in the Basque country. We found this dish in one of the many exciting tapas bars in San Sebastián, where they literally make the mayonnaise by the bucketful.

SERVES EIGHT TO TEN AS A TAPA, FOUR AS A FIRST COURSE

4 boneless chicken breast halves (about 4 ounces each), skin on
1/2 pound boneless, skinless chicken thigh meat
2 cloves garlic
One 1-inch slice good-quality French bread
1 large egg
Zest of 1 orange
1/4 teaspoon each salt and freshly ground black pepper
1 cup fresh mint leaves
1 teaspoon olive oil
1/2 cup dry white wine

ORANGE MAYONNAISE
1 whole orange, peel on, seeded and cut into small pieces
2 cloves garlic
1 large egg
1 teaspoon prepared mustard
1 cup olive oil
1/2 teaspoon salt

Working with one half-breast at a time, put the breast skin side up between pieces of waxed paper or plastic wrap. Using a kitchen mallet, pound the breast down and toward the edge of the meat so that the breast is as thin and wide as possible without tearing through the skin.

To make the stuffing, in a food processor or meat grinder, grind the thigh meat and put into a bowl. Finely mince the garlic and combine with the ground meat. In a small bowl, soak the bread in water to cover and squeeze dry. Combine with the ground meat along with the egg, orange zest, salt, and pepper.

Spread the chicken breasts on a work surface, skin sides down. Cover each breast with a layer of mint leaves, dividing them equally among the breasts. Divide the stuffing equally over each, flattening it over the entire breast. Roll each breast up lengthwise; tie with kitchen string at 2-inch intervals and once around lengthwise, twisting the string in the middle of the roll and going around the center of the roll. (Got that? If not, the point is simply to tie the rolls so they don't flop open while cooking.)

Coat the bottom of a heavy skillet with the olive oil. Over medium heat, add the chicken rolls, turning to brown them all around. Pour in the wine, cover, reduce heat, and simmer 25 minutes. Uncover, increase heat to high, and turn the rolls in the thickened juices until the pan is dry. Remove the rolls to a platter, cool, and refrigerate for 4 hours or overnight.

To prepare the orange mayonnaise: In a blender or food processor, grind together the orange and garlic. Add the egg and mustard and blend. With the motor running, gradually add the olive oil until a thick sauce has formed. Stir in the salt. Taste for seasoning. (The mayonnaise tastes better after refrigerating for several hours.)

To serve the chicken, remove the strings and slice each roll into thin rounds. Serve cold with the orange mayonnaise on the side, or put chicken rounds on slices of baguette and top each round with a dollop of the mayonnaise.

WINE SUGGESTIONS: The orange mayonnaise demands something a little different—perhaps a dry Gewürztraminer from California or Alsace. A more traditional choice would be a big, buttery California Chardonnay.

CRESCENT-SHAPED PASTRIES FILLED WITH CUMIN-SCENTED CHICKEN

Empanadillas de Pollo con Cumino

Empanadillas are a standard throughout the Spanish-speaking world. This version has a chicken-based filling, but there are vegetarian variations as well as those using seafood and other meats such as pork and beef. Let your imagination be your guide in creating your own fillings. In this recipe, the cilantro indicates that it is probably of Latin American origin.

SERVES TEN TO TWELVE

FILLING

3 tablespoons olive oil
1 pound boneless, skinless dark-meat chicken
1 teaspoon each cumin, salt, and freshly ground black pepper
10 green onions, trimmed of root ends
   and about one-third of the green part
1 cup minced fresh cilantro leaves

DOUGH

1/2 pound unsalted butter, softened
1/2 pound cream cheese, room temperature
1/2 cup cornmeal
3 cups all-purpose flour
Pinch each salt and cayenne pepper
1 egg beaten with 1 tablespoon water

To make the filling: Heat the oil in a medium skillet over medium heat and add the chicken. Sprinkle with the cumin, salt, and pepper and sauté about 10 to 15 minutes until cooked through. Remove the chicken to a work surface, roughly chop, and put into the work bowl of a food processor.

In the oil remaining in the skillet, sauté the green onions over medium heat until limp. Pour the green onions and any oil remaining in the skillet into the processor. Whirl just to finely chop without turning the mixture into a paste. Fold in the cilantro. Taste for seasonings and adjust according to your taste. The filling should be highly flavored and moist with the oil. Refrigerate the filling while you prepare the dough.

To make the dough: In the work bowl of a food processor, combine the butter, cream cheese, cornmeal, flour, and seasonings. Whirl to form a ball. Put the ball on a floured work surface and cut into quarters. Working with one section at a time, roll the dough out 1/4 inch thick and cut into 20 to 24 rounds with a 4-inch round cutter (an empty 7-ounce tuna can is perfect for this).

Divide the filling among the dough circles. Close the circles at the edges by folding in half, pinching together with your fingers. Cover and refrigerate for at least 1 hour (see Note).

To bake, preheat the oven to 400° F. Arrange the pastries on a greased baking sheet. Brush with the beaten egg and bake for approximately 30 minutes or until golden. Serve hot from the oven or at room temperature.

NOTE: The unbaked pastries can be frozen in one layer on baking sheets. When the pastries are frozen solid, pack in layers so they don't take up so much room in the freezer. Cover tightly with plastic. They will keep in the freezer for several months.

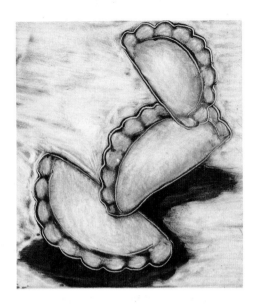

WINE SUGGESTIONS: This hearty snack can stand up to a rich, flavorful wine, either white or red. It is very good with an herbaceous Sauvignon Blanc and also matches well with a young Cabernet Sauvignon.

KEEPING SCORE

Many bars in Spain have zinc-topped bars. They are easy to clean and the barman often keeps track of drinks and food by marking the zinc with a piece of chalk.

Once, in a small town south of Seville called Arcos de la Frontera, we stopped to get out of the heat for a bit at a cool, shaded bar that looked inviting. It was also filled with locals—always a good sign. While we enjoyed glasses of *fino* sherry, an English couple came in, hesitant. They peered suspiciously at the mid-afternoon litter on the floor, but they finally settled themselves at the bar near us and ordered two beers and two small *bocadillos*, the ever-present Spanish version of a fast-food sandwich.

The English couple, perhaps recognizing the quality of the food, ordered several more rounds of beer, a tapa dish of grilled prawns, and a few other items as well. They polished off the prawns and the last of the beer. The woman fastidiously folded her paper napkin, then wiped away the crumbs from the bar in front of her, at the same time wiping away the chalk marks where the bartender had noted their orders.

The barman shook his head sadly and took a poll of the customers to calculate what the couple had ordered. Without cracking a smile, each customer responded with a long list of food and drink allegedly consumed by the English couple over the past thirty minutes.

The barman added it carefully on a pocket calculator, then showed the total to the couple. The final bill was staggering, probably more than the bar took in during an entire day. Their confusion was complete. The protests began. After a moment, the barman smiled a sly smile and announced that it was a free day for tourists and waved them away as the bar broke into laughter.

The couple, who a few moments before had been protesting at the size of the bill, now began protesting, in halting Spanish, that they must pay something. Very well, he shrugged, and reeled off exactly what the couple had ordered, to the peseta. Good will was restored all around and the English couple marched off into the afternoon sun, bewildered but convinced that they had just had an "authentic Spanish experience."

CHAPTER THREE

TAPAS PRONTO

Need something delicious whipped up in a hurry? Or something that you can make ahead for entertaining? There are plenty of tapas that fit either category—tapas that allow you to talk to your guests rather than requiring you to spend time chopping and grilling in the kitchen.

There are recipes throughout the book that could be *tapas pronto* or make-ahead tapas, but the following we have found to be especially quick and easy to make, either on the spot or for preparing in advance, from the simple but cheerful *Pan con Tomate* to our favorite for informal entertaining, *Tortilla Española*.

The sauces in chapter 4—*Mojo Rojo, Mojo Verde, Allioli* and *Romesco*—are also dynamite to have on hand. Any of them can make a piece of cold chicken straight from the fridge taste memorable.

GRILLED BREAD WITH FRESH TOMATO

Pan con Tomate

Bread and tomatoes: simple ingredients that taste fantastic, creating a whole that depends on absolutely the freshest tomatoes and chewy, crusty bread. This is a basic tapa all over Catalonia and the Balearic Islands, served at breakfast, lunch, dinner, and all points in between.

SERVES SIX TO TWELVE

6 thick slices French or Italian-style bread
3 fresh vine-ripe tomatoes
Salt
Extra-virgin olive oil

Grill the bread over a hot wood or charcoal fire until golden brown and slightly charred. Alternatively, put the bread under the broiler and toast it.

Cut the tomatoes in half. Rub one tomato half over each slice of bread. Rub and squeeze the tomato so that much of its pulp is deposited on the bread. Sprinkle a little salt and drizzle olive oil over each slice of tomato-drenched bread. Serve immediately. Absolutely delicious.

WINE SUGGESTIONS: A natural with a glass of *cava* or any light-hearted wine, such as a Beaujolais or a California Zinfandel, white or red.

PAN CON TOMATE

One bleak January morning, we visited a vineyard near the farming village of Arboc, in Catalonia, during the pruning season. The vineyard workers, who were taking a mid-morning break, had built a fire of old vines and were toasting rough slices of thick bread on sticks over the flames. When the bread was well smoked and slightly charred, a large tomato was cut in half and rubbed into the bread—*Pan con Tomate,* one of the most basic of Catalan tapas. Some of the workers added a thin anchovy filet to the bread, while others put on a few slices of chopped hard-boiled egg. This mid-morning snack was washed down by cups of rough red wine. The pruners had earned it. They had been in the field since first light, working steadily and skillfully in the biting cold to shape the vines exactly right, so that next summer's sun would warm the grapes into wine.

GRILLED MUSHROOMS WITH GARLIC & PARSLEY SAUCE

Champiñones a la Plancha

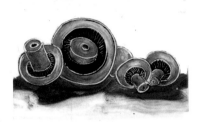

This not only makes a delicious hot tapa, but it is also
a perfect side dish with grilled meats. In the tapas bars
of Madrid, especially around the Puerta del Sol, grilled
mushrooms are served as a breakfast dish with scrambled
eggs. With a glass of light red wine, it is a favorite
wake-up call for Madrid's taxi drivers.

SERVES SIX

1/4 cup finely minced fresh Italian parsley
5 cloves garlic, very finely minced
6 tablespoons olive oil
18 large fresh mushrooms (about 1 pound)
Salt

Squeeze the parsley dry in a cloth or paper towel. Put it into a bowl with the garlic and moisten with 4 tablespoons of the oil. Set aside at room temperature for at least an hour.

Heat a heavy skillet or griddle over high heat. Pour in the remaining 2 tablespoons of oil and spread over the bottom. Put the mushrooms stem sides down on the hot surface. Sprinkle with salt. When they are nicely browned, turn the mushrooms and grill stem sides up until tender. Liquid will fill the mushroom caps; take care not to lose this when you transfer the mushrooms to a serving platter.

Top each mushroom with a dab of the parsley-garlic sauce and serve immediately.

WINE SUGGESTIONS: California Zinfandel, red please, goes very well with mushrooms. Pinot Noir is also a possibility, and as always with mushrooms, a dry *oloroso* sherry is lovely.

AVOCADO CREAM TOASTS

Tostadas al Aguacate

We had these delicious little bites at one of our favorite restaurants in Spain, Hierbabuena in Toledo. The flavor combination of avocado and cumin is an inspiration and is typical of the culinary treats being tossed off by some of the younger chefs of Spain. This tapa can be made a few hours ahead or quickly put together for unexpected guests.

SERVES TEN

1 large egg
2 cloves garlic
1 large ripe avocado
3 tablespoons freshly squeezed lemon juice
1/2 cup olive oil, plus additional olive oil for drizzling
1/2 teaspoon salt
Dash of cayenne pepper
2 teaspoons cumin seeds
1 long baguette, enough for 40 slices

Whirl the egg and garlic in a blender. Peel and seed the avocado, cut it into chunks, and add to the blender along with the lemon juice. Whirl until smooth. With the motor running, slowly add 1/2 cup olive oil. Season with the salt and cayenne. Cover and refrigerate until ready to serve, but no longer than a few hours.

Preheat the oven to 400° F.

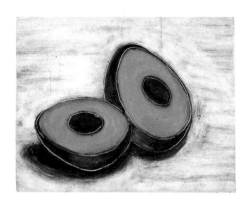

Toast the cumin seeds in a hot, dry skillet over high heat until they begin to dance across the pan. Turn the seeds out onto a plate and set aside.

Thinly slice the baguette into about 40 rounds. Arrange the slices on a baking sheet and drizzle with olive oil. Bake for about 12 minutes or until golden brown.

At serving time you can either spread some of the avocado cream on each slice of bread and sprinkle with the toasted cumin seeds, or put the cream in a bowl, sprinkle the seeds over it, and serve surrounded by the toast slices for dipping.

WINE SUGGESTIONS: Chardonnay seems to have a natural affinity for the richness of avocado. Here, match strength to strength with a toasty, buttery Chardonnay that has a firm lashing of oak.

WHAT IS A TORTILLA?

A rose may be a rose and all that, but a tortilla is not necessarily a tortilla. It was a point of great confusion for customers at our Spanish tapas restaurant, Cafe Tango, in the late 1980s. Naturally, *Tortilla Española* was on the menu, but like most Californians, many of our customers were far more familiar with Mexican food than Spanish.

Just what, they wanted to know, was *Tortilla Española* all about? Some neglected to ask before ordering and expected to get the flat, round corn or wheat flour-based Mexican tortillas. They were quite surprised at the thick, creamy, potato omelet, which most resembles a frittata, that appeared.

POTATO & ONION CAKE

Tortilla Española

This most traditional of tapas satisfies in a homey, nurturing way. In Spain, workers often take their early-morning breaks with a slice of *tortilla* and a *cortado,* a cup of strong Spanish coffee just lightly cut with milk. Or, later, they break for a glass of red wine and top a slice of grilled bread, maybe *Pan con Tomate* (page 84), with a hunk of *tortilla* and eat it like a sandwich. *Tortillas* are always available in tapas bars and are usually a good choice. Because they taste so creamy, we are often asked if *tortillas* contain cheese—they don't. A very simple dish, *Tortilla Española* depends absolutely on the very best ingredients. This is an ideal make-ahead tapa. Accompany with *Allioli* (page 102).

ONE 8-INCH TORTILLA; SERVES 12 TO 16 AS A TAPA

1/2 cup olive oil
3 medium onions, peeled, quartered,
   and sliced 1/4 inch thick
Salt and ground white pepper
4 medium russet potatoes (about 4 pounds), peeled,
   quartered, and cut 1/4-inch thick (see Note)
6 large eggs, beaten

Heat the oil in an 8-inch nonstick or cast-iron skillet. Add the onions, sprinkle with salt and pepper, and cook over medium heat until soft, about 15 minutes. Pour the onions and oil into a strainer set over a bowl. Return the strained oil to skillet. (Leave onions in the strainer so more oil can drain from them.)

Reheat the oil in the skillet, add the potatoes, sprinkle with salt and pepper, and cook over medium heat, tossing occasionally, until they are golden and a little crunchy, about 15 minutes.

Drain the potatoes in a strainer set over a bowl and return the strained oil to the skillet.

In a bowl, combine the onions, potatoes, and eggs. Reheat the oil in the skillet (there should be about a tablespoon or less). Pour in the egg mixture. Cook the *tortilla* over medium-low heat until set on the bottom. It will still be runny on the top. Cover the skillet with a lid or a flat, rimless pizza pan, quickly invert the *tortilla*, and just as quickly slide it back into the skillet. Cook until the *tortilla* is set. When you press the center of the *tortilla* it should have a little give, and the sides should be firm.

Turn the *tortilla* out onto a platter and let rest about 15 minutes or longer before serving. If you refrigerate the *tortilla*, bring it back to room temperature or heat it briefly in the microwave before serving.

NOTE: When preparing the potatoes, peel and cut them just before using to prevent discoloring. The potatoes should not be put in water to hold, as this will destroy the potato starch that helps to give a creamy quality to the finished *tortilla*.

WINE SUGGESTIONS: You need a wine with good acid balance to match the creaminess of the *tortilla*. A French Chablis or a glass of California Sauvignon Blanc should work well. If you insist on red wine—and why not?—a California Merlot could be very good here.

HAM & CHEESE CROQUETTES

Croquetas de Jamón y Queso

In this version of the popular Spanish tapa, use good-quality ham so that its flavor comes shining through. This is an excellent make-ahead dish, as is the version using tuna on page 38.

SERVES SIX TO TEN

$1/3$ cup unsalted butter
$3/4$ cup all-purpose flour
$2/3$ cup cold milk
$1/4$ teaspoon each nutmeg and freshly ground black pepper
1 cup chopped ham
1 cup $1/4$-inch cubes Swiss cheese
1 teaspoon chopped fresh parsley
1 cup fine dry bread crumbs
1 large egg
Vegetable oil for frying

In a small saucepan, melt the butter and stir in $1/4$ cup flour. Cook and stir over low heat for about 1 minute. Add the cold milk all at once and continue to stir over low heat until thickened. Stir in the nutmeg, pepper, ham, cheese, and parsley. Pour the mixture into a pie plate and thinly spread it out. Cover with waxed paper and refrigerate until firm.

Put the bread crumbs and remaining flour into two separate, deep-sided flat plates. Beat the egg in a bowl with 1 tablespoon water.

Form the ham mixture into 28 balls, about 1 heaping teaspoon each. One ball at a time, drop first into the flour to coat, then into the egg to coat, and lastly into the bread crumbs. Gently shake or rotate the plates of crumbs and flour to evenly coat the balls.

Put the croquettes onto a baking sheet and refrigerate until cold. They can be cooked immediately or kept, refrigerated, until the next day. You can also freeze the croquettes, spread apart on a baking sheet. When frozen solid, pop into a plastic bag and keep in the freezer for up to six months. They can be fried as needed, still frozen.

To cook the croquettes, heat oil 2 inches deep in a skillet or use a deep-fat fryer heated to 380° F. When the oil is hot, carefully drop in a few croquettes at a time and cook until golden (exact cooking time will vary, so watch carefully). Drain on paper towels and serve immediately.

WINE SUGGESTIONS: Ham and California Sauvignon Blanc go together like—well, like ham and eggs. Also lovely with a rosé from Spain's Rioja district or a glass of Spanish *cava*.

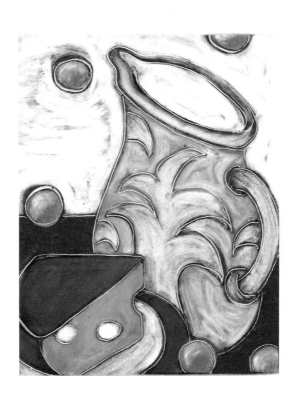

THE MOJO CONNECTION

There are as many versions of Canarian *mojo* sauce as there are Canarian cooks—probably more, since each cook might have a basic repertoire of green and red sauces, plus versions with several levels of heat.

Although *mojo* is more common in the Canary Islands than on the mainland (which is how the islanders refer to European Spain), we actually ran across it several years before visiting the Canaries at a riverside tapas bar in Seville. However, it is an exotic on mainland Spain.

Perhaps this is because the use of cilantro, a native herb of southeast Asia and India, has never really taken root on the mainland, even though it was first brought to Spain by the Moors. Canarian cooks, however, have taken to cilantro as no other Europeans, save the Portuguese, have. No doubt its popularity is a result of centuries of trade between the islands and Central and South America, where cilantro was probably introduced by Asian traders before Columbus.

Although chile peppers are not a major ingredient of *mojo*, they are used to add nuance and finish to

many of the sauces. There are dozens of peppers grown in the Canaries that are seldom found on the mainland. Again, this is an example of the close ties between the islands and Latin America. Many Canary Islanders go to Latin America looking for work and end up staying several years before returning to the islands with enough cash to start a small business or buy a home. Besides the cash, they also bring back pepper seeds. A quick walk through a Canarian cook's kitchen garden will reveal peppers from virtually every country in Latin America, and the cook usually has a *mojo* recipe for each pepper.

Working with the basic *Mojo Verde* sauce it is possible to use different combinations of peppers, a little parsley, maybe some basil, and become a major *mojo* center yourself. So get your *mojo* working.

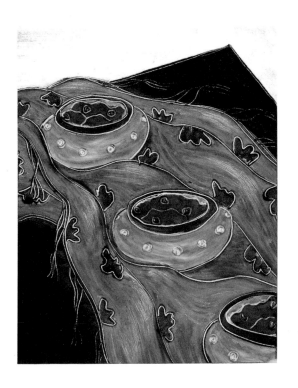

CHAPTER FOUR

TAPA SAUCES

These sauce recipes can be used with dozens of tapas to delight and astound the most jaded palate. *Allioli* and *Romesco,* the two basic Catalan sauces, supply zest to any tapa or main dish. The Canary Island *Mojo Verde* and *Mojo Rojo* add to the complexity and diversity of your sauce battery.

Put a pot of each of these sauces on your tapas buffet and you'll notice guests becoming very inventive about how to use them. In fact, finger food takes on a whole different dimension. Using these sauces as a framework, you can turn the simplest selection of foods into a fiesta.

Here are some suggestions:

- Use *Romesco* or *Mojo Verde*
  to brighten shellfish dishes.

- Enliven wedges of *Tortilla Española* or raw
  vegetable pieces with a dollop of *Allioli.*

- Top grilled eggplant or broiled chicken
  with *Romesco.*

- Try either *Mojo* or the *Allioli* sauce for working wonders
  to a simple plate of boiled potatoes, grilled fish,
  or steamed asparagus.

ALLIOLI

Allioli is a deceptively simple sauce—you could think of it as a kind of garlic mayonnaise—that adds a richness and texture to grilled meats, especially lamb and rabbit, but also works beautifully with grilled chicken, fish, prawns, and bits of stale bread for a quick snack. In its purest form, *allioli*, sometimes spelled *alioli*, is simply garlic and olive oil, but it comes together much easier with the addition of one or two egg yolks.

If the sauce should separate, pour the sauce into a spouted jar or other container. Add 1 tablespoon water and ¼ cup of the separated sauce to the blender and, with the motor running, gradually add the remaining sauce. It should set right up.

Allioli can easily be made by hand. In Spain, it is typically made with a mortar and pestle and beaten until the pestle stands straight up in the mortar without falling over. *Allioli* made by hand has a rougher texture and a darker color than machine-made *allioli*.

SWEET RED PEPPER, TOMATO, & HAZELNUT SAUCE

Romesco La Bleyda

This sauce is based on a *romesco* from a rustic restaurant called El Merendero in the tiny village of La Bleyda, which is at the end of a red dirt road outside Villafranca del Penadés in Catalonia. There are never more than three or four dishes available at El Merendero, including grilled chicken or fish, which are delicious with this sauce. In the spring, they serve *calçots*, a vegetable similar to a young leek, with *romesco*. You peel the outer leaves off the *calçot* and dip it in the *romesco*. It can get wonderfully messy.

MAKES ABOUT 3-1/2 CUPS

1/2 cup hazelnuts
6 large cloves garlic, unpeeled
3 medium tomatoes
1 thick slice white bread
1 large red bell pepper
1/2 cup olive oil
1/4 cup red wine vinegar
1/2 teaspoon each salt, freshly ground black pepper,
*   and red pepper flakes*
1 teaspoon paprika

Preheat oven to 400° F.

Put the nuts, garlic, and tomatoes on a baking skeet and bake in the oven for 15 minutes.

Toast the bread in a toaster or under the broiler. Coarsely chop and set aside.

Roast the bell pepper over the open flame of a gas stove or under a broiler until all the skin is charred. Put the pepper into a plastic bag, close the top, and let sit for 10 minutes.

Remove the nuts, tomatoes, and garlic from the oven. Peel the garlic, and rub the nuts between towels to remove the loose skin (it's not necessary to remove all the skin). Put nuts, toasted bread, and garlic in a food processor and pulse until finely chopped.

Peel and quarter the red pepper and halve the tomatoes. Add to the nut mixture and pulse briefly to combine. With the motor running, pour in the oil and vinegar. Add the seasonings and pulse until smooth and well combined.

Pour into a container, cover, and allow to rest for a few hours for the flavors to meld. Serve at room temperature. Tightly covered, the sauce will keep for two or three weeks in the refrigerator.

GREEN SAUCE
Mojo Verde

This bright green sauce probably came to mainland Spain
from South or Central America via the Canary Islands,
where we enjoyed it with virtually every meal. It is exciting
to both the palate and the eye. Explore its uses with other fish,
meat, and cooked vegetables such as boiled potatoes, or as
a lively dip for raw vegetables.

MAKES ABOUT 2 CUPS

4 cloves garlic
1 cup fresh cilantro leaves
1 medium green bell pepper, stemmed and seeded
1/2 cup olive oil
2 tablespoons red wine vinegar
Salt and pepper to taste

In a blender or food processor, whirl the garlic with the
cilantro until it forms a paste, carefully pushing the solids
down with a rubber spatula. Cut the bell pepper into small
pieces; add to the blender with the olive oil and vinegar and
whirl until smooth. Season with salt and pepper. Let rest for 30
minutes before serving. This sauce will keep for several hours
but turns a little gray if kept overnight.

RED SAUCE
Mojo Rojo

This delicious sauce (often served alongside
Mojo Verde) is especially tasty with pork.

1 ancho chile
1 cup fresh cilantro leaves
3 cloves garlic
4 sprigs fresh thyme, leaves only
1/2 teaspoon salt
1/4 teaspoon ground cumin
1/2 cup olive oil
2 tablespoons red wine vinegar

Put the chile in a small bowl and cover with boiling water. Let
rest, covered, for ten minutes, then drain and remove the stem
and seeds but do not peel.

Combine the chile, cilantro, garlic, thyme, salt, and cumin
in a food processor. With the motor running, add the oil and
vinegar and thoroughly blend. The sauce can be kept covered
in the refrigerator for up to one week.

INDEX

TABLE OF EQUIVALENTS

The exact equivalents in the following tables have been rounded for convenience.

US/UK	**Metric**
oz=ounce	g=gram
lb=pound	kg=kilogram
in=inch	mm=millimeter
ft=foot	cm=centimeter
tbl=tablespoon	ml=milliliter
fl oz=fluid ounce	l=liter
qt=quart	

Oven Temperatures

Fahrenheit	Celsius	Gas
250	120	1/2
275	140	1
300	150	2
325	160	3
350	180	4
375	190	5
400	200	6
425	220	7
450	230	8
475	240	9
500	260	10

Liquids

US	Metric	UK
2 tbl	30 ml	1 fl oz
1/4 cup	60 ml	2 fl oz
1/3 cup	80 ml	3 fl oz
1/2 cup	125 ml	4 fl oz
2/3 cup	160 ml	5 fl oz
3/4 cup	180 ml	6 fl oz
1 cup	250 ml	8 fl oz
1 1/2 cups	375 ml	12 fl oz
2 cups	500 ml	16 fl oz
4 cups/1 qt	1 l	32 fl oz

Length Measures

1/8 in	3 mm
1/4 in	6 mm
1/2 in	12 mm
1 in	2.5 cm
2 in	5 cm
3 in	7.5 cm
4 in	10 cm
5 in	13 cm
6 in	15 cm
7 in	18 cm
8 in	20 cm
9 in	23 cm
10 in	25 cm
11 in	28 cm
12/1 ft	30 cm

Weights

US/UK	Metric
1 oz	30 g
2 oz	60 g
3 oz	90 g
4 oz (1/4 lb)	125 g
5 oz (1/3 lb)	155 g
6 oz	185 g
7 oz	220 g
8 oz (1/2 lb)	250 g
10 oz	315 g
12 oz (3/4 lb)	375 g
14 oz	440 g
16 oz (1 lb)	500 g
1 1/2 lb	750 g
2 lb	1 kg
3 lb	1.5 kg